Countess Markievicz
An Adventurous Life

Written by Ann Carroll
and illustrated by Derry Dillon

IRELAND'S BEST KNOWN STORIES IN A NUTSHELL

Published 2016
Poolbeg Press Ltd

123 Grange Hill, Baldoyle
Dublin 13, Ireland

Text © Poolbeg Press Ltd 2016

A catalogue record for this book is available from the British Library.

ISBN 978 1 78199 870 0

Cover design and illustrations by Derry Dillon
Printed by GPS Colour Graphics Ltd, Alexander Road, Belfast BT6 9HP

This book belongs to

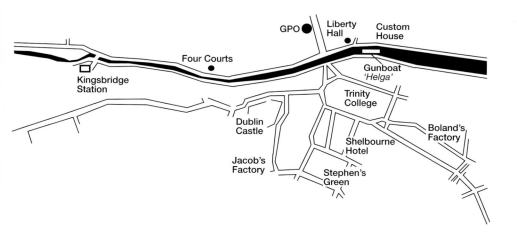

Available in the Nutshell Myths & Legends series

The Children of Lir
How Cúchulainn Got His Name
The Story of Saint Patrick
The Salmon of Knowledge
The Story of the Giant's Causeway
The Story of Newgrange
Granuaile – The Pirate Queen
Oisín and Tír na nÓg
The Story of Brian Boru
Deirdre of the Sorrows
Heroes of the Red Branch Knights
The Adventures of the Fianna
The Adventures of Maebh – The Warrior Queen
Diarmuid and Gráinne and the Vengeance of Fionn
Saint Brigid the Fearless
The Vikings in Ireland
Journey into the Unknown – The Story of Saint Brendan
The Story of Tara
Niall of the Nine Hostages

Poolbeg are delighted to announce that some of our Nutshell titles are now available in Irish

Available now

Childhood

Born in 1868, Constance had the perfect start in life.

She was the eldest of the rich Gore-Booth family, with two brothers and two sisters, and grew up in Lissadell, a great house overlooking the sea in County Sligo.

Her sister, Eva, was her best friend, though they were very different.

"How is it we get on so well?" Constance asked once. "You love poetry and reading, where I like galloping through the woods and hunting and shooting! The only time I stay still is when I'm painting."

"You love adventures, Con, and I love hearing about them," Eva told her. "And it's good to watch you paint – your pictures are so vivid. And we both love Lissadell and its people."

Tenants

The people Eva was talking about were the tenants who rented land from their father and lived in cottages on the estate.

They've all got lots of children and very little room, Constance thought.

Both girls were fascinated by the stories they heard about the Great Famine.

"Your father was good to us during the hard years," one tenant might say. "He didn't let us starve when the potatoes failed."

"That's what happened to the poor Daly family in Coolaney, Lord have mercy on them," his wife would add. "Their children died and the mother soon followed with a broken heart."

"And what about the O'Haras?" the man would note. "All of them were driven off the land and into the workhouse because they couldn't pay the rent – a fine neighbourly family who surely deserved a better land-lord!"

Then both would quickly say, "But your father now, he was a good landlord. We've no complaints there, so we haven't, oh God no!"

Constance and Eva began to understand how privileged their lives were.

Leaving Home

Part of such privilege meant the sisters were painted by famous artists and that, aged nineteen, Constance was presented at court to Queen Victoria.

Later on, she decided to study Art, first in London and then in Paris.

There she fell in love with a handsome young Polish count, Casimir Markievicz, who was a painter too.

"He's already married," she sighed, "and has a small son. I should try to forget him."

But Casimir's wife grew ill and died and, three years after they met, he and Constance married.

Irish Freedom

They settled in Dublin with his young son, Stanislaus, in 1903. By this time their daughter, Maeve, was born but the child was raised by her grandparents in Lissadell.

One day, Constance's childhood friend, the famous poet William Butler Yeats, called to her Dublin house.

"Do you know anything about Maud Gonne?" he asked.

"I know she's a famous beauty," Constance said, "and I know you're mad about her and you're always writing poetry for her!"

"Someday I may write poetry for you too,"
Yeats said. "But did you know Maud has set
up a women's group called The Daughters of
Ireland? They want this country to be free
from British rule."

"I'd like to join that movement," Constance
said. "If Ireland had self-rule, there'd never
be another famine and people would have
a fairer life!"

Joining

So Constance met Maud Gonne and arranged to go to a meeting of The Daughters of Ireland. However, she was invited to a ball on the same night at Dublin Castle, which was the centre of British rule.

Constance loved a party and thought: Sure I can go to both! I'll slip away from the ball, make the meeting and be back before the last dance!

But when she arrived at the meeting, the other women weren't a bit impressed by her tiara and shimmering gown.

"Will you look at that get-up!" one muttered. "What's she doing here dressed like that?"

"The state of her! Wearing a crown!" said another.

But Constance must have impressed them, for she managed to join the movement.

The Cause

The Countess had found a cause she loved: Irish Freedom.

When King George V came to Dublin in 1911, she joined the protests against the royal visit and for the first time she was arrested and sent to gaol for a short time.

But not even gaol could stop her now.

Before this, in 1909, she had set up Fianna Éireann, a Scouts movement named after the famous ancient band of warriors, The Fianna. She told the boys, "I'll take you camping, train you as soldiers and teach you how to use guns. One day you'll be ready to fight for Irish freedom."

She was true to her word and seven years later Pádraig Pearse, the leader of the Volunteers in the Easter Rising, would say, "Without the Fianna, no Rising would have been possible."

Some of the boys Constance had trained fought in the rebellion, while the younger ones carried messages between the rebel garrisons. A few lost their lives, caught in crossfire or hit by snipers.

The Lockout

But, before this, when the bosses locked workers out of their jobs in 1913 for wanting to band together in a trade union, there was no doubt whose side Constance was on.

She knew James Connolly and joined The Irish Citizen Army, set up by him to protect the workers.

"How can I help?" she asked.

"We need to do something for the workers'
families before they starve, Con," James told
her. "We have the worst slums in Europe. Did
you know there are 107 people living in one
house in Henrietta Street? It's a disgrace! And
now because there's no work, there's no mon-
ey and no food!"

So Constance used some of her wealth to set up a kitchen in Liberty Hall and provide food for all who needed it.

And although the workers had to give in and sign a promise not to join a union, in the long run they won the rights they wanted.

Gun Running

The plans for a rebellion were hotting up.

When guns were brought from Germany into Howth Harbour on a yacht, the *Asgard*, in 1914, Constance was among those waiting for them.

She and some of her Fianna boys helped to unload rifles and ammunition onto wheelbarrows and carts.

Rumours had reached the police and they turned out in force, but Constance and the others managed to get most of the guns away to safety.

Now the rebels had weapons.

"Did you hear what happened after you were gone, Con?" a friend later asked Constance. "A crowd gathered and the police fired on them because they were jeering and throwing a few stones. Three were killed!"

"Things will have to change soon!" Constance was more determined than ever.

1916

Constance made a flag to fly over the GPO – the General Post Office in Dublin – when Pearse took over the building on Easter Monday 1916. It was actually a green bedspread! On it she painted 'Irish Republic' in gold. But she didn't have enough paint so she had to get some mustard from the kitchen and mix it with the paint to make it stretch! Unfortunately, her cocker spaniel Poppet took a fierce dislike to this work of art and tore off a large corner.

On the day, Pearse read the *Proclamation of the Irish Republic* outside the GPO. Already the other leaders had taken their troops to set up garrisons all over the city. The Rising was under way.

"It's a pity our Chief of Staff tried to cancel the Rising!" Pearse said. "Many were confused and didn't come. But those of us who turned up will hold out against the British Army. Then the people will join us, and victory will be ours!"

Constance was second-in-command to Michael Mallin in Stephen's Green.

Snipers in the Shelbourne Hotel tried to pick the rebels off. The Countess gave them something to think about with her return fire.

Surrender

But, in spite of the trees and bushes, there wasn't enough cover and so they took over the College of Surgeons on the opposite side of the Green.

Here they held out for six days.

However, by then O'Connell Street, the GPO and the surrounding streets were in ruins.

"My reports say too many people have died," Pearse mused. "And there's no sign of the people rising. Now, with the British gunboat *Helga* on the Liffey, shelling the city, there can only be more destruction. It's time to call a halt!"

Pearse sent out the order to surrender and personally surrendered his gun and sword to the British General Lowe.

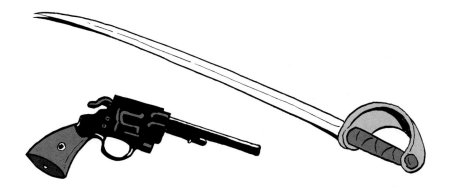

Prison

Jeered by the crowds, the captives were marched away from the College of Surgeons by Captain Wheeler and his troops. The captain was married to a cousin of Constance.

Constance was held in Kilmainham Gaol and sentenced to death, but later an officer was sent to inform her, "Because you're a woman your sentence is commuted to life imprisonment."

Constance was disgusted. "I wish you had the decency to shoot me!" she told him.

Now each day, from her prison cell, she could hear the shots as the leaders of the Rising were executed and she wished she could share their fate.

Instead she was sent to Aylesbury Prison in England.

Excitement Over?

Around this time Constance wrote to her sister, Eva:

"All my days seem to have led up to the last year. It's been such a hurry-scurry of a life. Now I feel I have done what I was born to do . . . and I can slip back into a quiet pool of the sea."

But there were no quiet times waiting for Constance.

A Different Ireland

All the rebels were freed in 1917 and Constance came back to a different country.

The executions of the Easter Rising leaders had turned the people against the government and now they lined the streets to cheer her homecoming.

She was the first woman elected to be a
member of parliament in the British House
of Commons, but she refused to take her
seat. Instead, when Sinn Féin set up an Irish
government in 1919, she became Minister for
Labour – the first and only woman minister
for another sixty years!

Ireland was settling into a kind of peace.

1922: Civil War

Then came the Treaty and after that the Civil War.

"I want an Irish Republic of 32 counties and cannot settle for 26!" Constance swore. "This treaty signed with the British is wrong!"

So she took the Republican side against the Free State and fought under the leadership of Éamon de Valera.

"Civil War is the saddest kind of war," she soon realised. "Brothers, families, old friends, all turning against each other and killing those they once loved."

Eventually the Free State won.

Someday all of Ireland will be free, Constance thought. But for now I'm glad the bitter fighting is over.

Death

When Éamon de Valera set up the Fianna Fáil party in 1926, Constance joined and was again elected.

Then she suddenly fell ill and went into a public ward in Patrick Dun's hospital.

By this time she had given away all of her wealth to help the poor, who mourned her loss when she died five weeks later, surrounded by shocked family and comrades.

She was refused a State funeral by the Free State Government, but crowds lined the streets to say farewell and de Valera spoke at her grave in Glasnevin Cemetery.

In Memory

Yeats' poem 'In Memory of Eva Gore-Booth
and Con Markievicz' describes the young
sisters:

Two girls in silk kimonos, both

Beautiful, one a gazelle.

Constance was the gazelle.

In 'Easter 1916', he remembered her as a
great society beauty, born to a life of wealth:

What voice more sweet than hers

When young and beautiful

She rode to harriers?

But Constance believed in fairness and
could never have settled for a life of privilege.

The End

All you need to know about Ireland's best loved stories in a nutshell

Also available in the series

The Story of Newgrange

The Salmon of Knowledge

The Story of Saint Patrick

How Cúchulainn Got His Name

The Children of Lir

The Story of The Giant's Causeway

Granuaile The Pirate Queen

Oisín and Tír na nÓg

The Story of Brian Boru

Deirdre of the Sorrows

Heroes of the Red Branch Knights

The Adventures of the Fianna

The Adventures of Maebh The Warrior Queen

Diarmuid and Gráinne and the Vengeance of Fionn

Saint Brigid the Fearless

The Irish Vikings

Journey into the Unknown The Story of Saint Brendan

The Story of Tara

Niall of the Nine Hostages

ORDER ONLINE from poolbeg.com